FE[...]

OF

FAITH

Time to cast off

Cyril & Gabrielle

Thomas

This book is dedicated to our children,

Kayti, Gareth, Natasha and Sian,

who made many sacrifices as teenagers and young people

to support us in our journey of faith.

CONTENTS

ACKNOWLEDGEMENTS

We want to express our thanks to family and friends who have encouraged us in the writing of this book. We are especially grateful to Liz Tingman for proofreading the text and making very helpful suggestions for improving it.

Introduction

This little book is intended to encourage, inspire and challenge those who desire to follow the Lord Jesus Christ wherever He leads and be at all times submitted to His word and the direction of the Holy Spirit.

The apostle Paul reveals that the revelation of Christ in us as "the hope of glory" is a key to accessing the glorious riches of a mystery that has been kept hidden for ages and generations (Colossians 1:26-27). Our lives as disciples of Jesus Christ will not sink into a humdrum, dull routine of shallow existence when we realise that within us something glorious, eternal and heavenly has been divinely implanted. Our destiny is to be ultimately reached through revelation of God's secret wisdom that He destined for our glory before time began (1 Corinthians 2:7).

Sadly the pressure to remain confined by the challenges and insecurities of daily life and allowing our actions to be conditioned by the wisdom of this age can prevent us from enjoying life in the heavenly dimension.

God will give grace, courage and strength to the fainthearted who dare to trust Him and commit themselves to full obedience and simple discipleship. The Christian life was always meant to be radical. Hopefully this book will provide some practical help from the lessons that we have learned as we have sought to follow the direction of the Holy Spirit.

Part One is autobiographical and is an account of how God graciously called us and set about sorting out our messed-up lives so that we could serve Him as a married couple working alongside one another on the mission field.

Part Two is a collection of prophecies given in recent years to us in the south west of Ireland where we have lived following our retirement from the work in China. Each prophecy is usually followed by an example of how truths contained in the prophecy were fulfilled in our previous experiences.

Part Three is a collection of our most recent prophetic words emphasising the radical challenge which we believe God is making to His church today, calling His beloved bride into a more intimate relationship with Him.

Part Four is intended to encourage all who love the Lord to find release from whatever may be preventing them from using the gifts which He has placed within them and to be aware of our sacred responsibilities as we grow in prayer, intercession and worship.

We trust that readers will be blessed as they prayerfully consider what we have shared and apply whatever God may be speaking to them. It is our intention if God enables us to publish further books to share more of our experiences and prophetic words from our spiritual journey on the mission field in China and elsewhere. We are praying and believing for an end to the ever-tightening restrictions being placed upon Christians by the current government of the People's Republic of China. We are hopeful that we shall be able to provide more detail of locations and events in future publications as we have attempted to be very sensitive to the safety of our Chinese colleagues in this book. The light of the gospel continues to shine in the darkness and will eventually overcome it (John 1:5).

Part One

Our Journey

"You are like a person who has left the safety and security of the river bank and stepped into the boat moored alongside. It's time now to cast off from the river bank and to move out into the middle of the river. I have prepared currents to take you forward to the destinations that I have chosen for you but you have to make the decision to put your trust in Me and cast off. You cannot see the way ahead in the darkness but as you let Me direct the passage of the boat so you shall find peace, joy and fulfilment.

The longer you stay where you are, lingering in the shadows, fearful of casting off from the security of where you have been, the greater will be the sense of unease and frustration. Trust Me. Just as I have prepared a boat for you so that you did not have to plunge into the cold water, so I have prepared the way ahead for you. Boats are designed to move along in the water not to stand forever still. Use the boat for what it was intended. Start moving."

Our spiritual journey was birthed in the mind of God long before we were born. As we look back over our lives, we can see that the presence of God has always been there even when we were determined to go our own way and not even acknowledge His existence. He is ever loving and faithful, the Good Shepherd who calls His sheep by name and draws them with wounded hands of love from the dark places where they have sunk, sometimes powerfully using His rod and staff to bring them out of dangerous pits of mud. Only the pride of man would deceive him into thinking that it is better to run with no clear sense of direction along dark pathways than to walk in the light of God's presence.

We met as students when we were full of all sorts of ambitions, fantasies, insecurities, pride, prejudices and uncertainties. We had each gone to university thinking to find out for ourselves what life was all about and to realise our potential. We both knew very quickly after meeting one another that we had met the person with whom we would share the rest of our lives. Love blossomed very quickly and we married and started a family while we were still young.

There is a vast difference between the relatively self-centred life of a student with few responsibilities and the life of parents trying to manage a household on one salary. We entered into marriage like most people as damaged individuals, trying as best we could to handle all the challenges and still stay together and hold onto our initial love for each other. We had started married life praying together but faith ebbed away at times with the challenges of a growing family and frequent moves necessitated by the demands of a professional career.

Our individual journeys of faith experienced twists and turns but generally the path led downwards into depths of doubt and cynicism, a reflection inevitably of the deteriorating quality of our relationship as a married couple. Within seven years, disillusionment with marriage and church life led Gabrielle into a position where she declared that she was an agnostic. Cyril, having tried unsuccessfully to maintain commitment for a season to a traditional Pentecostal church, reached the conclusion that he still believed in the Christian faith but the best that he could manage was living as a worldly churchgoer. We were both honest about where we were spiritually and this was a positive place to be for God hates pretence. It is when we are willing to look at ourselves and realise what we are that God is able to start bringing circumstances and events to confront us with the reality of Himself.

On the second day of February 1972, having left England the previous day, we arrived in Hong Kong, excited, apprehensive but delighted to be stepping out of the ordinary, pedestrian, predictable life that had become humdrum and confined into what we believed would be a totally life-changing, enthralling new world of experience. It certainly was but also initially challenging and very different from we had expected.

By this stage we had four children and Cyril had taken advantage of an unexpected opportunity to embark on a full-time study course lasting almost three years to become a Chinese interpreter specialising in Cantonese. Prior to this

Cyril had left the United Kingdom only once previously as a teenager to visit Germany; he was completely unprepared for acute jet lag and consequent sleepless nights coupled with extreme culture shock and feelings of insecurity.

Added to the stress of this was mounting anxiety about finance and how the family would cope plus the tension as he realised that the Chinese language with its tones and characters is one of the most difficult in the world to master. For some months we had no home of our own but had to manage living in two rooms in a hotel near the racecourse. In sharp contrast Gabrielle felt that she had come home as she relished the freedom that comes with entering a whole new panorama of a refreshingly different world.

As Cyril struggled to come to terms with stress-filled sleepless nights he came to the realisation that there was only one possible solution: prayer. In front of his agnostic wife he got down on his knees and bargained with God: "If you will get me out of this mess, I shall do anything you want me to do." Is it not the case that God will often use the crises and desperate situations, that are often the result of our own choices, to bring us to the place where we can see no way forward, no escape route? We cannot give ourselves fully to the Lord until we first surrender our wills. His thoughts and ways are not ours; we are not naturally inclined to abandon the right to choose the direction for our lives and make our own decisions. The pathway to Christian maturity can often only be walked by those whose stubborn wills and self-importance have been broken on the anvil of affliction.

The answer to the prayer came: sleep-filled nights, gradual improvement of our financial situation, the eventual provision of a three-bedroom apartment and consistent progress in the study of both oral and written Chinese. God was certainly getting us out of the "mess" but what was it that God wanted of us?

There was certainly no change in our pattern of life and Cyril felt no urge to adjust his worldly form of churchmanship. However, shortly after Cyril's cry for help to God, the minister of an English-speaking congregation, who was desperately trying to recruit an organist and choirmaster and, hearing that Cyril had some experience, implored him to fill the position. In spite of great reluctance and fearing that such a commitment would use precious time for Chinese language study, Cyril responded positively, assuming that this would be the "anything" that God required of him. He was to discover that the pathway of obedience is a step-by-step process that begins with small acts of surrender, learning to trust that God will bless and make provision for every need, always encouraging us to continue moving forward on the journey of knowing Him and discovering our real selves on the way.

The early seventies were a glorious season in the spiritual development of the universal church with the outpouring of the Holy Spirit which became known as the Charismatic Renewal. Speaking in tongues or glossolalia, prophecy and other gifts of the Holy Spirit, described in the New Testament, were being experienced by both Roman Catholic and Protestant Christians. Prior to this they had been usually only present in the meetings of Pentecostal churches following a similar outpouring of the Holy Spirit at the beginning of the twentieth century in Los Angeles. Sadly the Pentecostal movement, which had grown rapidly, had splintered into a number of denominations who often viewed each other suspiciously; exercise of the gifts of the Holy Spirit was occasional and meetings could be lacking in spontaneity. A common feature of the Charismatic Renewal was the emergence of meetings and fellowships in private homes where people from various church backgrounds met in a relaxed atmosphere of informality where there was an expectation that speaking in tongues and prophecy would be a central feature of the meetings.

Cyril and Gabrielle had their first experience of the Charismatic Renewal at a meeting that took place on Thursday evenings in the home of the deputy headmaster of one of the large international schools on Hong Kong Island. It was led by an American couple, Rick and Jean Willens, and participants included Jackie Pullinger, who subsequently became famous for her work among Chinese drug addicts, David Aikman, the *Time Magazine* journalist and author, as well as people representative of the diverse international and Chinese population crowded into what was still a British colony. Meetings were unpredictable but unthreatening with people free to share their testimonies, pray, speak out using the gift of tongues or give prophetic revelation. Cyril felt particularly challenged as he realised that his brand of worldly churchmanship was totally lacking in the power to enable him to lead a life consistent with the demands of Christ. Gabrielle was intrigued by the meetings but felt no reason to change from her firmly held agnosticism.

On the 25th February 1973 Gabrielle as was her custom once a month attended the Anglican church where Cyril was the organist and choirmaster and the three oldest children sang in the choir. She came quite reluctantly to the formal, traditional service which followed a set liturgy simply because we needed to travel as a family after the service to a lunch served monthly in the colonial-style army officers' mess in Lyemun Barracks overlooking the South China Sea.

The church, a picturesque white building, was a British army garrison church situated in the far end of the Stanley Peninsula where the King's Regiment from Liverpool was stationed. Before reciting the set prayers for intercession, the army chaplain shared that a soldier from the regiment had died following months in a coma caused by being shot while on duty in Northern Ireland, leaving behind a widow and family. From the depths of her being Gabrielle cried out in protest against the seeming futility of such a tragedy: "Why, God, why?"

What happened then left her reeling emotionally, her mind in shock, as God responded in an audible voice: "Don't fight any longer. Come home." Her spirit recognised immediately the voice of her heavenly Father but her mind struggled to come to terms with accepting the fact that the God, whose existence she had ceased to believe in, was there drawing her to Him with cords of purest love.

It was not until the early hours of the next day that Gabrielle was able to explain to Cyril what had happened during the church service. What followed then was an acceleration of significant events as they made their first tentative efforts to pray together after a lapse of many years, conscious that God was beginning to do something profound within them that could not be contained within the limits of conventional behaviour. Cyril was made aware of this when he realised the same day that all desire for cigarettes had gone and he was totally free of his addiction with no effort on his part. He was deeply aware too that he lacked the will power and strength to commit his life to Christ knowing how emotionally unstable he was and susceptible to peer pressure. The solution was clear and simple: he needed the power of the Holy Spirit as Jesus had made clear to his disciples following the resurrection:

"But you will receive power when the Holy Spirit comes on you; and you will be my witnesses in Jerusalem, and in all Judea and Samaria, and to the ends of the earth." (Acts 1:8)

Intellectually knowing is one thing but a willingness to abandon the right to please yourself as to how you live your life is very different. Why do we struggle to abandon what we imagine to be the freedom to make our own choices instead of handing over our twisted, confused lives to the loving Creator whose desire is that we should know the freedom of living as His chosen children, beloved, secure, voyaging on a journey of discovery that transcends the dimensions of time and space? God is infinitely good and living within His kingdom will mean leaving behind the darkness of being imprisoned to self, sin, fear, guilt, low expectation and deception.

Attendance at the Thursday evening charismatic meetings became a regular feature of the week for us as we took tentative steps to respond to the supernatural encounter which Gabrielle had experienced in Stanley Fort garrison church. Following the close of the meetings in the spacious lounge of the deputy headmaster's house, there was usually opportunity for those desirous of being baptised in the Holy Spirit to withdraw to one of the smaller rooms where they could receive prayer and have hands laid upon their heads. The evidence of the Holy Spirit's filling the seeker and imparting divine power was the ability "to speak in tongues", to talk in a language that had never been spoken previously by the seeker. Cyril was extremely reluctant to seek this experience for a number of reasons: he had found that his upbringing in a Pentecostal family and church had caused him to feel very negative about much of what he had observed; he had no confidence that he could break through layers of inhibition to feel sufficiently released "to speak in tongues"; he feared losing control. However, having previously indicated his interest in being baptised in the Holy Spirit he found himself in the awkward position of not being able to refuse when some enthusiastic members of the group offered to pray with him at the close of one of the meetings.

Two young Americans, Bob and Hal, sat either side of Cyril in the small room and laid hands on his head after encouraging him to pray aloud and ask God to fill him with His Holy Spirit. Bob and Hal continued with fervent prayer using their gift of tongues while Cyril inwardly froze feeling an intense sense of embarrassment. Eventually Cyril suggested that they should stop as he was simply feeling acutely self-conscious and had no inclination to speak in tongues. Bob and Hal responded by saying that they had unlimited time and were very happy to continue praying for him until the breakthrough came. They encouraged him to open himself to God and, as he felt a stirring within, to recognise that this was Holy Spirit beginning to fill him; he had only to respond by opening his mouth and begin praying, not in English, but to launch out with whatever sounds came into his mouth.

Breakthrough came as Cyril realised in desperation that there was but one course of action before him: to believe what had been said and in faith start to speak out in an increasingly loud voice whatever words his mouth formed. A wonderfully exhilarating torrent of words poured from his lips as he declared praises to God in a fluent outpouring in a language which he was speaking for the first time; there was no doubt Cyril had been well and truly baptised in the Holy Spirit.

The days and weeks that followed for us were remarkable, with Gabrielle receiving prayer a week later for the baptism of the Holy Spirit, an experience which for her was a much quieter, less dramatic one. Joy bubbled within them as they were overwhelmed with intense feelings of love that flowed in new depths between them and outwards to others around them. There were painful experiences too as they realised that the Holy Spirit activated within them a desire for absolute truth; this meant facing up to failures in previous years when their marriage was encountering challenging times and being honest with one another about those failures. We discovered that at the heart of successful marriage is a commitment to the Lord, truth, the other partner, the word of God, praying together and a determination to seek first the Kingdom of God. The Spirit-filled life is never a shallow one and the Spirit-filled marriage is never a dull one. The Holy Spirit explores the depths of a yielded vessel, bringing forth treasure from hidden places and transforming a life of bondage to self-centred cravings to Christ-centred aspirations.

The baptism of the Holy Spirit and the joy that flows with growing into the fullness of living in Christ are not experiences that God graciously bestows simply for our own comfort and edification. Gifts of the Holy Spirit are given to be channelled outwards so that the fruit of the Spirit-filled life might draw others to Jesus. Increasingly self must decrease and the Lord must increase as sensitivity to the needs of others grows. To live a Spirit-filled life is to live a disciplined life, a life totally submitted to the direction flowing from the throne of God as awareness grows of the need to discern the thoughts and ways of our heavenly Father.

Within weeks of receiving the baptism of the Holy Spirit, we were approached by another member of the Thursday evening charismatic prayer meeting, Jackie Pullinger, who had pioneered a ministry of reaching out to Chinese criminal heroin addicts in the notorious Kowloon walled city. There had been a breakthrough with Triad gang members in the Chaiwan resettlement estate on Hong Kong Island. Resettlement estates had been built as a fast response by the British authorities to the housing needs of thousands of Chinese refugees who had fled Communist China in desperation; each family was given one room and had to share communal toilet facilities. Crime, drug addiction and Triad gangs featured strongly in these densely populated areas where families struggled with the demands of daily living in an international city, a swirling microcosm where the extremes that revolved around wealth, poverty, glamour, exploitation, finance, nightclubs, prostitution, superstition, ambition, intrigue, tourism and political uncertainty gyrated constantly in hypnotic motion.

Jackie needed another Cantonese speaker to commit himself to the work in Chaiwan so that she could be released to give herself to the needs of the walled city in Kowloon. In committing ourselves to helping the drug addicts of Chaiwan, we did not realise that this step of obedience to what the Lord was asking of us would result in a progression of further steps of surrender to Him and abandoning much that had seemed so important previously. Our home became a refuge for drug addicts seeking freedom from addiction and the weekly outreach meetings in Chaiwan developed into a ministry with two full-time Chinese workers who needed support. Cyril's professional colleagues, British middle-class people with little real contact with the local Chinese population, were not impressed, with the result that his career prospects were seriously damaged.

The pathway of surrender and obedience to the King of kings never comes to an end in this life. It is the only way to experience fully the joy, peace and fulfilment that God desires to lavish upon His chosen ones. In 1979 having been transferred to a new position in the south of England, we came to the realisation that it was time to relinquish any expectation of pursuing a normal career path in order to embrace the calling of God to full-time service in China.

The call had come four years earlier when we were praying one morning in our bedroom in Colchester where we were living temporarily between work assignments in Hong Kong. As we worshipped the Lord, singing songs in English and the gift of tongues, Gabrielle was transported in the Spirit back to Hong Kong and across the South China Sea to the mainland of China and landed in a large city in southern China. She was shown the main features around the city, given four Chinese words and assured that we would be returning there to work. The Chinese words, in Mandarin, meant nothing to either of us. At that time China was a closed nation to foreigners following the Cultural Revolution which had brought the cessation of all church activities and the closure of all places of worship. It was not until some weeks later when Gabrielle had opportunity to look at a large atlas that she discovered that two of the Chinese words were the name of a provincial capital city in southern China that she had visited in the Spirit.

Following the death of Chairman Mao Ze Dong, the Chinese communist paramount leader, in 1976, the Chinese nation under new leadership slowly and very cautiously started to open the door that had been closed to most of the world since the Communist Party took control in 1949 following a brutal civil war. At that time we were back in Hong Kong committed to a life of total obedience to the Lord Jesus Christ, involved in a number of church-related activities in the time available when Cyril was not doing his secular job. Shortly before leaving Hong Kong for a new position on Salisbury Plain in the south of England in 1978, it came to our knowledge that it was possible to visit the city in China which Gabrielle had already visited in the spirit.

We travelled there as members of a closely monitored tour group organised by the Chinese government, saddened to observe a nation that seemed to have slept in a colourless, drab time warp dating back decades under the repressive control of the communist authorities. We were delighted to meet people whose spirits had not been crushed by suffering, and awestruck to discover that the city, a provincial capital, corresponded exactly to the one that Gabrielle had been shown previously.

Knowing that God had called us to China overrode all other considerations which meant embracing challenges and sacrifices not only for us but also for our four teenage children who were remarkably supportive. Since our baptism of the Holy Spirit in 1973 we had developed the practice as a family of praying and worshiping together, sharing concerns, questions and direction that any of us were receiving. Resigning from Cyril's secure position meant relinquishing a salary, diminished pension prospects, a large comfortable residence and a first-class education for our children in a picturesque, fee-paying boarding school. Committing ourselves to a life of faith and trusting the Lord to supply every need necessitated moving into a small Victorian cottage that had been empty for some time. As space was limited, we had to sleep on a sofa bed in the lounge so that the children could have the bedrooms upstairs. The three younger children had to adjust to a large comprehensive school in a town some distance away, a school with pupils from all social classes so different from the privileged middle-class world of the English fee-paying boarding school. There were undoubtedly great challenges with adjustments having to be made and managing on a greatly reduced income but in it all there was a great sense of joy, adventure, togetherness, expectation and fulfilment in knowing that we were responding to the call of God upon us as individuals, a married couple and a family.

The big question facing us as we took steps to move forward in God's call to serve Him in China was knowing the direction to take in facilitating that call. The door for service in China was only just beginning to open and we realised that it could take some time before ministry there was possible. Chinese Christians had suffered years of persecution by the communist authorities with many being imprisoned for years and some being martyred. It was impossible to know what was left of the Chinese church that had been established by foreign missionaries and developed in the century before the Communist revolution of 1949.

We had not been shown the nature of the work which we would be undertaking in China. All we knew was that we needed to prepare ourselves. It seemed clear to us that the first step was to return to Hong Kong as missionaries; Cyril was fluent in Cantonese and we had a wide circle of friends in the missionary community there. The advice we received was to take the route of ordination in the Anglican Church and return as members of the Church Missionary Society. Prayerfully we followed this advice and were accepted for ordination training by the Church of England and placement by the Church Missionary Society, a course of action which necessitated two years' training for ministry in an Anglican theological college in a historic cathedral city in the south of England.

Many were surprised that we had taken the route of ordination in the Church of England; although we had served in various roles over the years in Anglican churches, we were much more comfortable ministering in informal, unstructured group meetings where there was freedom for all to participate and exercise charismatic gifts. Even more surprising was our choice of theological college which was liberal in its theological emphasis and tending towards high church or inter-faith practices in its churchmanship.

From the beginning of the two-year course, Cyril was involved in confrontative situations with the hierarchy when he refused to participate in humanistic activities and challenged lecturers who undermined the authority of the Bible. A typical example of the spiritual state of the college was the decision to invite Maurice Wiles, Regius Professor of Divinity at Oxford University and contributor to the notorious, liberal "The Myth of God Incarnate," to deliver the Holy Week Lectures in 1980. Cyril was often a lone voice in challenging the assertions made by such respected academics and clergymen in their undermining the truth of the word of God. He was often the object of hostile criticism and told that his narrow approach was contrary to what was presented as authentic, broad-church Anglicanism and was threatened at one difficult meeting with expulsion.

At the same time appreciation and respect grew from members of staff and fellow ordinands as they observed our disciplined approach to prayer and fasting, the exercise of charismatic gifts and commitment to mission. The two years of study and release from secular work were a wonderful season of preparing ourselves for the mission field, growing together as a couple and as a family, and becoming more aware than ever of the realisation that without a solid foundation in the word of God we would not be equipped to confront the challenges that would be facing us in Communist China.

As the time for completion of the two years' training for ministry approached, we were informed by the Church Missionary Society that a new bishop had been appointed in Hong Kong and we could not be placed there for the time being. The CMS urged us to continue with our plan of joining; it would arrange a position in another part of the world until one became available in Hong Kong. The offer was very attractive: financial security, accommodation, provision for all our family's needs and a pension plan. We knew, however, that God had called us to China, to a life of obedience and trust in Him to provide whatever we needed in the assurance that He is a faithful God.

The summer of 1981 was indeed for us a colossal exercise in moving forward in the life of faith. Cyril's fellow students were all preparing for ordination to serve as curates in various parishes where salaries and houses were waiting for them. We were stepping out into a void as, having closed the door which the Church Missionary Society had graciously opened, all attempts to secure a paid teaching position in Hong Kong were fruitless. Our finances, which had just enabled us to provide for our needs while Cyril was at theological college, were exhausted. Increasingly we sensed that God was directing us to move out in faith and travel back to Hong

Kong in the expectation that He would open a door for us and take care of us as a family. We were also coming to terms with the fact that our eldest daughter, who was only 19, had become engaged to a delightful young man, who was also graduating from college that summer, and they were going to marry after his graduation prior to moving to Cornwall where a permanent job was waiting. His parents had very kindly suggested that we shared the wedding expenses. The bottom line was that we needed to cover our share of our eldest daughter's wedding and, as soon as possible afterwards, purchase five, one-way air tickets to Hong Kong for the rest of the family.

The life of faith is intended to be challenging. God will allow us to be tested so that trust in Him can grow and character be developed. Of course, we need to be certain that we have truly heard from Him and are not being presumptuous. There needs to be complete unity as there was with us and our children. Nothing should be attempted that is contrary to scripture. Others, whom we respect in the body of Christ, will confirm too the visions and prophecies which have been received, and most of all we need to be experiencing the all-surpassing peace of God.

We were truly blessed to have the spiritual support of the apostolic leadership of a vibrant group of independent fellowships that had been birthed in the charismatic renewal of the 1960s onwards; at their annual summer conference in Cliff College in the Derbyshire Peak District, George North and Norman Meeten laid hands upon us and prayed for us following our declaration that we were obeying the call of God and moving to Hong Kong. Truly we needed to be absolutely certain that we had heard from God as we took radical steps: selling our car and all our possessions to purchase one-way air tickets as well as giving up our rented cottage with no guarantee of where we could live for an extended period. In addition, there was the seemingly irresponsible decision to remove our three teenage children from school and college not knowing what provision there would be in Hong Kong. Cyril, in view of all his experience with teaching and academic work, found this particularly challenging but felt an assurance from God that He was responsible for the children's future, not Cyril. We praise God that all of our children have been blessed with successful marriages, rewarding careers, meaningful contributions to Christian mission, and academic achievements including university degrees and a doctorate.

We flew from London Heathrow Airport on 18 August 1981, two adults and three teenagers, with six suitcases, one suitcase each for our personal belongings and the sixth containing everything that we possessed, mainly practical items like cooking utensils and towels. Our total wealth was about one hundred pounds. We carried no credit cards. We did not know where we would live, what we would do or how we would support ourselves when we arrived the next day in Hong Kong's crowded, bustling Kaitak airport. God is absolutely faithful and trustworthy. We had stepped out in faith, knowing that God had entrusted us with a vision but the fulfilment would only be realised as we continued trusting Him and continuing on the journey of faith wherever it would take us. Sadly many, who are entrusted with visions, callings and prophetic words, never see their fulfilment because of an unwillingness to step out of comfortable living and security to put their complete trust in the Lord who has promised to move mountains in response to faith. Many are indeed called but few are chosen. We were delighted and relieved to be met on our arrival in Hong Kong by friends who escorted us to spacious accommodation in a luxurious apartment complex in the south of Hong Kong Island. It was the home of another family who were out of town and eager for us to make it our temporary home, and so provision continued for several weeks as we moved to squeeze into the apartment of another family who very kindly invited us to share their home while we waited on God to clarify our long-term ministry and his provision for us.

It is of paramount importance that we do not delay in responding to His call upon our lives. We shall discover that timing is vitally important because there are people, circumstances and events that in the plan of God are dependent on our being in the right place and the right time for His purposes to be outworked. Shortly after arriving in Hong Kong we were introduced to a family from Australasia who had served the Lord on the mission field in Asia and in church pioneering in Australia over many years. They had settled in Hong Kong a year or so previously, believing that they were called to launch a new ministry. For the time being they were serving in a large missionary organisation with its headquarters in Hong Kong but really were waiting for others to join them so that the launching of the new ministry would be undertaken by a team who would be able to combine their gifts and experience. The vision for the new ministry was large and would require immense resources and a growing international team of men and women willing to move in faith and obedience, submitted to the word of God and willing to be accountable to one another. At the heart of the ministry would be a community of believers open to the Holy Spirit and growing in the life of God, committed to evangelism and outreach, and willing to take the gospel to the rest of Asia.

We were very excited to meet Paul and Bunty Collins who were well known in charismatic circles internationally, particularly in Australia and New Zealand. They had a wealth of experience and, like us, were eager to see the gifts of the Holy Spirit in operation. Paul was a gifted preacher and evangelist which complemented Bunty's impressive gift as a Bible teacher. They were pleased to meet us too as we brought with us enthusiasm, dedication, prophetic giftings, fluency in oral Cantonese and written Chinese, wholesome family life and the trust of many in Hong Kong's church and professional circles. The four of us connected well and were thrilled to discover that we had all been drawn to the outlying island of Lamma, which we felt would provide the base for the ministry to be established.

The fishing village of Sok Ku Wan had no church but it had a temple and a plethora of fresh seafood restaurants which were a popular destination in the evenings and weekends for Chinese and foreigners living in the crowded urban areas of Kowloon and Hong Kong Island. No Westerners lived there which meant that, unlike most of Hong Kong, accommodation could be rented at reasonable cost. Within weeks of returning to Hong Kong, we collected our few possessions together and moved out to an empty house that Paul and Bunty had rented outside the village on a steep hillside. The local community were astounded to see a Western family moving into their Chinese village and probably very surprised that unlike most foreigners had so few worldly possessions. We soon discovered why the house had never been lived in: it was adjacent to a graveyard and the villagers were terrified of ghosts. We saw no ghosts but plenty of mosquitos who filled the house where we were sleeping on the floors. The first evening in the eery emptiness of the vacant, mosquito-filled, isolated house brought us face to face with the reality of the enormity of the steps of faith that we had undertaken in abandoning the safety and comfort of our former life style. On such occasions we can succumb to doubt and depression or we can, like Paul and Silas in the Philippian prison, start praying and singing praises to God. As we sang and opened ourselves to the presence of God, our spirits were lifted. What a joy it was to awake the next morning and look across a beautiful, sunlit valley in the knowledge that we were running the race that the Lord had ordained for us.

With Paul and Bunty and their family moving a short time later into the small, Spanish-style, three-storey villa, it became necessary to find alternative accommodation for our family of five. Gabrielle felt directed by God to focus upon a two-storey, older property on the waterfront overlooking the bustling line of seafood restaurants. She felt that it had been impressed upon her that there were Chinese characters written on the building; it was only after careful scrutiny that Cyril discovered that underneath the layer of white paint there was indeed a line of Chinese characters which stated that the premises were the South Lamma Gospel Hall. On making enquiries we were told that many years previously there had been an evangelical church there but it had closed when the pastor emigrated. God was leading us to reclaim lost territory.

Having made contact with the landlord, the local ferry owner, we were able to view the upper floor which was in a shabby, disgusting state following its previous use as a working men's dormitory. The challenges involved in moving into such a place were formidable as partitions would need to be made to create bedrooms, there was just one filthy toilet and no bathroom, in addition to the fact that the superstitious villagers were hostile to our taking up residence as our Christian presence would upset the local spirits.

To become overcomers will involve us in many struggles, challenges and a willingness to continue moving forward in faith. So often the first challenge will be our own fears, prejudices and inhibitions which will need to be dealt with if we are to live in the reality of being able to do all things through Christ who strengthens us (Philippians 4:13). We need too to be able to exercise the authority which has been entrusted to us. In this case the protracted reluctance of the local ferry owner to let the premises to us was finally overcome when he realised that we were determined to rent the premises and move in without further delay. His agreement was finally secured on the condition of our paying an unrealistically high rent every month; very aware of our lack of income and any financial resources, we agreed trusting God that His limitless resources would provide whatever was needed.

In our experience God moves in response to the obedience of His servants to do whatever He is calling them to do and their willingness to take steps of faith. We and the Collins family were the first Westerners to move to Sok Kwu Wan to take the initial steps in establishing the Siloah Ministry. We were thrilled to be rapidly joined by others from across Hong Kong and various countries who were eager to be part of what God was doing, to respond to the ministry, to participate in meetings where there was a flow of worship and gifts of the Holy Spirit and where there was the opportunity to be fulfilled in the outworking of the vision.

Some came faithfully in the evenings and weekends, travelling by ferry from Kowloon and Hong Kong Island, for the Bible teaching and lively meetings; others came to live in places that we rented for them on the island to become members of the community. Within the next year or so a range of activities had been launched: training programmes especially for young people, mission teams being sent out internationally, a local church established for the Chinese community, drug rehabilitation in conjunction with Jackie Pullinger and a conference in a central Anglican church in Kowloon. In less than two years Siloah had become an established ministry in Hong Kong, supporting other ministries and events, and attracting others in ministry from overseas to join us or be connected with us in the exciting work that God was doing.

It seemed for a season that the momentum of what the Holy Spirit was doing in us and through us was unstoppable. Increasing numbers were joining us at our meetings as well as those coming from overseas to take up residence near us on Lamma Island. The long-term vision was ambitious: the building of a complex of purpose-built meeting places, offices and accommodation in the centre of the island. Scripture encourages us to have the faith to move mountains secure in the knowledge that nothing is too difficult for God.

Scripture also cautions us that we are to be careful how we build for "the fire will test the quality of each man's work" (I Corinthians 5:13). Sadly within less than two years Siloah was shattered with the ministry divided and people confused, upset and leaving to find fulfilment elsewhere. The root cause was, as is often the case with church divisions, a lack of unity within the core leadership, between the Collins and us. Over the years we have observed that the cause of disunity in many church divisions is rarely doctrinal but usually a clash of personalities.

There were obviously precious lessons to be learned. We certainly needed to search our own hearts and examine our motivation and actions with a willingness to repent of anything done or said that was not an expression of the love of Christ. In coming together with Paul and Bunty we had moved very quickly to form the new ministry with little time to appreciate and grow in understanding of differences of background, attitudes, Biblical interpretation, church practice and values. Siloah was an independent ministry with no outside accountability or oversight which meant that when differences in the leadership arose there were problems in resolving them. In the years that followed we made it our policy in forming our ministry to China that we should always be accountable to an international board of experienced, mature, Godly men who could be relied upon to help resolve problems involving the leadership.

Splits and divisions within churches and related ministries, like a family breakup, are devastating for all involved. Most of us have high expectations of Christian brothers and sisters; as relationships are developed, our trust levels rise. When differences emerge and people find themselves in irreconcilable camps, so often the worst in human nature is manifested.

The Siloah split was one of our most painful experiences as harsh words were spoken, accusations levelled and friendships suddenly shattered. During the height of the storm that raged as our world seemed to fall apart, the Lord assured us that He was teaching us precious lessons that could not be learned from books or the experiences of others but only as we trusted Him to take us through the pain and sense of loss.

What were the lessons? Obviously the differences between the Collins and us should have been addressed much earlier before the ministry was allowed to mushroom and others joined us in leadership. If mutual trust and friendship between leaders are being eroded the foundation of any work is increasingly weakened. Collective leadership is challenging but where "brothers live together in unity…the Lord bestows His blessing, even life for evermore" (Psalm 133). Sadly many ministry and leadership teams function like secular professional ones; there is fellowship but shallow friendship and an avoidance of issues which should be addressed if church communities are to experience the effervescent life that God desires for them.

Another vital lesson was that all of us and especially those in leadership positions need to examine our desires, motivations and ambitions. Are we in danger of using people and organisations to further our goals and ambitions? Do we react to criticism in an aggressive way because of insecurities that are being exposed within us? The emphasis in the gospels and the New Testament epistles is upon the overriding importance of love, not successful ministry. True shepherds really care for the sheep, are interested in the sheep and are self-effacing, not mindful of their own importance and status. God will allow all work done in His name to be tested in the fire of internal and external challenges; that which is not bearing the fruit that He desires will be discarded while that which is will be subject to pruning and refining. The testings of God will include marriages, friendships, meetings, ministries, churches, programmes, prophecies and visions. That which comes through the fire will be purer, sharper, more effective, more compassionate, wiser, deeper, stronger and closer to the heart of God. The split within Siloah and its eventual collapse, painful as it was, made clear to us that our focus was to be upon what God had called us to do in China and to continue with outreach to the local Chinese community on Lamma Island. We were thankful that others with the same motivation remained committed to us so that these ministries continued. We were thankful too that broken friendships were eventually restored in the months and years that followed as issues that had been controversial were clarified.

Within a year or so Paul and Bunty left Hong Kong for ministry in other parts of South East Asia and Australia. It has been a blessing to meet with them in subsequent years and to put the past behind us, maintain contact, and express our love and appreciation for one another. We were determined to remain on Lamma Island, knowing that God had led us there and that the vision which we had been entrusted with for outreach in China was undiminished. Shortly before the eruption within the Siloah ministry, we had felt guided by the Lord to Mo Tat Wan, a small, picturesque hamlet about half an hour's walk along the coast from the main fishing village where we had been living. For about eighteen months we had come to enjoy the challenges of life above the oyster sauce factory in our makeshift apartment but now we were being invited by local residents to consider renting an attractive three-storey residence that had been recently constructed overlooking the beach. It had everything that we could desire: bedrooms for our teenage children, spacious lounges with sea views, bathrooms, accommodation for co-workers, a flat roof, space for an office and access to a ferry. Taking on responsibility for renting the house was another enormous step of faith as we had no salary but it was vital that we took the step as this house and other accommodation became the base for our ministry into China for the next fifteen years or so. Over these years hundreds of people from around the world came there to be commissioned for service across the border, for ministry, team meetings, baptisms and fellowship.

Since returning to Hong Kong in 1981 in response to the Lord calling us to serve Him in China, we had not lost our focus upon the provincial capital in southern China where Gabrielle had been taken in the Spirit seven years earlier and which we had visited in a closely monitored tour group in 1978. Remarkably an American missionary organisation had been flooded with requests from the same city for English-speaking pen pals as a result of a television advertisement. On hearing of our commitment for outreach there, the American missionary responsible for the programme passed on to us a long list of names and addresses of people in the city who had been in contact.

Prayerfully we selected as many names as we could and handed them on to the young people attending our training programme in Siloah to write to these Chinese people and inform them that we would be visiting the city and would enjoy meeting them. The result was that when we returned to the city in 1982, making our own way this time, not as members of a tour group, we found people waiting and eager to meet us. Most of them were teachers or students, eager for conversation in English as few of them had ever met a foreigner before. The city was still very drab but significant changes had taken place since our previous visit four years earlier. The church had been allowed to re-open, the only one in a city of half a million. We learned from the pastor that he had been forced to work as a labourer for decades. Many of the older people whom we befriended had suffered appalling abuse during the horrendous Cultural Revolution that Chairman Mao had inflicted upon the nation during the 1960s and 1970s.

We had to move carefully knowing that we were being watched but Cyril's fluency in the language enabled us to get around the city and meet people in their own homes and other locations. Deep friendships were started that continued long afterwards and wonderfully, Bibles, which were difficult to obtain in China, were eagerly received. Our new friends were obviously very open to the gospel and very appreciative of the opportunity to study the word of God.

Very encouraged by the enthusiastic welcome and responses of our new Chinese friends, we returned to the city a few months later, staying in a newly constructed, multi-storey hotel by the large river near the centre of the city. We never tired of exploring the city, walking along the tree-lined avenues teeming with bicycles, talking with any who wanted to engage in conversation with us. Many of our new friends were lecturers or students at one of the many university campuses that for the most part were situated in the west of the city. Prayer was an important feature of our days, either seeking guidance in our hotel bedroom or walking the streets. One morning as we sought to know the Lord's will, we were given a prophetic word which told us that a door would be open for us that day and we were to walk through it. Shortly afterwards the telephone rang; one of our new friends, a young university lecturer, informed us that his faculty wanted to invite us to give all its students a lecture about studying English. This was an incredible breakthrough. Instead of being suspicious foreigners, we were suddenly transformed into important visitors, driven from our hotel in an official-looking black car with dark lace curtains into the middle of the university campus. We were ushered into an unbelievably shabby lecture hall, packed with students who were eager to hear at last a native English speaker. Cyril gave his lecture to a very appreciative audience, drawing on his years of experience as a language teacher. To Gabrielle's horror, the head of the faculty was so appreciative that he insisted that Gabrielle gave a talk too.

The breakthrough continued as the next day we were invited to visit another university to give a similar lecture to the English lecturers. On this occasion Gabrielle felt it right to stay back at the hotel praying while Cyril spent the morning at the university. He returned with the head of department who wanted to offer us a teaching position. A similar offer was forthcoming from the other university. Doors were being opened. It was so important that we had been in prayer and knew what the Lord's strategy was for the next phase. Having prayed for the city and doors opening for seven years, Gabrielle was initially bewildered when Cyril informed the university authorities that we would be unable to take up the academic positions offered but would recommend a suitable teacher.

We had great responsibilities in Hong Kong within the leadership of Siloah as well as a family to care for which would have made a move very difficult. More importantly Gabrielle was reminded the words of Jesus in John 12:24: "I tell you the truth, unless a grain of wheat falls to the ground and dies, it remains only a single seed. But if it dies, it produces many seeds." She realised that we could have gone to work in mainland China at that stage but there would just have been the two of us. If she was prepared to let her ownership of the vision die, with us being at the centre of it, then God would multiply it. It was true that we could go, teach and the Lord would enable us to do a good work but it would just be the two of us. On returning to Hong Kong and sharing news of the invitation with our Siloah fellowship, we were delighted that a young, gracious woman who had recently graduated from an English university willingly volunteered to become the first teacher we were to send into China. She was amazingly brave. The accommodation on the university campus was basic with simple furniture and no bathroom but was luxurious compared with the homes of the local staff members.

There were only two other foreigners in the city and neither of them were Christians. Anne would need to depend on the Lord for strength and encouragement every day. Communication with us and others was very limited as there were only a few telephones in the university offices; visits from us and others in the fellowship in Hong Kong could only be occasional. In a country devastated by years of political struggle, cultural uniformity and religious persecution, the life of Christ radiated through this young woman's serenity and joy causing hope to rise in flattened souls and drawing them to the giver of life.

The collapse of the Siloah ministry, as in all church splits, had both negative and positive outcomes. A positive consequence for us was that we were free to give ourselves to developing the work in China, birthed in vision and prayer, and now taking root with sending a teacher to live and work on a university campus. We have observed over the years that although it has been sad, painful and often traumatic to lose people who have chosen to separate themselves from us and our ministry, the result has been usually growth and increased fruitfulness. We have therefore made it our policy never to try to hold on to people who were no longer comfortable working with us. Obviously on such occasions we have had to search our own hearts and ask the Lord to cleanse us from any wrong attitudes and motivation, to refine and purify us, to be sure that we were walking in the light. Unity in any ministry is vital as Psalm 133 emphasises. When a group of Christians are committed to prayer and working through differences in a spirit of humility, love and unity, blessing will inevitably flow and fruitfulness will increase. We were privileged over the years to have a small team of people from various countries and churches living, working and praying alongside us at the base on Lamma Island. We were also able to make ourselves accountable to an international team of directors who could oversee the China ministry.

In one of the parables of the Kingdom of God, Jesus compared it to a tiny mustard seed being planted in the soil and subsequently growing into an extremely large tree with branches big enough to attract many birds of the air. One of the authentic hallmarks of the operation of the Kingdom of God is increase and growth. Having died to a personal ownership of the vision and planted a tiny seed in a large city in China, we witnessed rapid growth. The lifestyle and teaching of our teacher, Anne, her respect for the authorities and care of her students so impressed her superiors and colleagues that requests flowed for more English teachers from other academic institutions around the city. Within a few years we were able to establish a team of about a dozen teachers from UK, USA, Canada, Australia and New Zealand who were able to join in fellowship and support one another.

In our discussions with university authorities in the city, it became apparent that every aspect of life in China was dominated by the Communist Party; individualism was not a factor to be considered as all life was viewed from a collectivist viewpoint. This viewpoint fitted well into historic Chinese patterns of behaviour which have been shaped by the teaching of Confucius with its emphasis on respect for authority and the traditional large Chinese family.

The university authorities were suspicious of us not just because we were foreigners but because we did not seem to belong to any organisation or unit as they termed it. It was indeed a fact that with our Charismatic background and wanting to be led by the Holy Spirit and not be conformed to human organisations, we had set about placing teachers in Chinese academic institutions with that mindset, hoping that the strength of friendship and fellowship would keep us in harmony. However, it became clear that progress could not be made in negotiations with Chinese officials if we were not able to present ourselves as having a corporate identity.

It is, of course, imperative in the outworking of any vision there is flexibility in allowing events, circumstances and the opinions of others to shape the structure that develops. For us it meant the establishment of an association, legally registered in Hong Kong, with its own bank account, which would eventually become a non-profit-making, charitable organisation with a board of directors.

Church history is replete with many examples of people with great vision and faith who have pioneered church organisations and missions which grew quickly into institutions with large followings. Sadly so often the sense of vision and pioneering faith has been lost as others have taken over management of the organisations and their operation have been dominated by regulations and financial considerations. The pioneering leaders may discover that eventually they are an embarrassment to the work they founded and find themselves excluded.

Our aim with the growth of the ministry in China has always been to maintain the life of the Holy Spirit and the emphasis on prayer. We have welcomed people from a wide variety of church backgrounds as long as they have had a personal experience of salvation and respected the authority of the Bible. We have been delighted that the sense of family has never left the work nor has the willingness to engage in open, frank discussion to work through differences and find a way forward. Life in the Holy Spirit can ebb and flow in the lives of individual believers and churches. It can never become something mechanical which can be turned on automatically by gifted musicians, impressive preaching or the use of tongues, helpful as all of these can be in opening us to the spiritual realm.

Jesus said that God desires people to worship Him in spirit and in truth (John 4:23-24). The gentle dove which personifies the Holy Spirit will move on if there is an absence of complete truth and integrity. We were determined that as individuals and as an organisation we would never abandon honesty and transparency, particularly as our dealings with officials in the People's Republic of China increased and we became aware of the corruption that was endemic there.

It has been our experience that life in the Holy Spirit can start to diminish when the life of faith decreases and reliance on human resources increases. The apostle Paul was able to say that he was being renewed inwardly day by day because he was able to fix his eyes "not on what is seen but on what is unseen" (2 Corinthians 4:16-18). From 1983 onwards the number of teachers that we were sending into China increased and the awareness of the hand of God upon the work notwithstanding all the challenges that most pioneering mission organisations face in such areas as financial needs, misunderstandings, resignations and tensions in relationships.

There was also expansion in the number of locations where we were asked to place teachers, from universities in remote locations in the far North West to academic institutions in vast metropolises like Beijing and Shanghai. As our teachers sought to be salt and light in their new communities, many of them were drawn to visit children's welfare centres where large numbers of babies and young children were placed as a direct consequence of China's harsh one child per family policy. Our decision to approach the leadership of these welfare centres and declare our willingness to take on responsibility for caring for abandoned children in units that we would furnish, equip and staff was an enormous step of faith. The opening of these doors as well as the cooperation and friendly attitude of welfare centre and local government officials was awesome and truly an amazing answer to faithful, persistent prayer.

The story of how we came to open and run three residential children's homes, day centres, programmes for youngsters with special needs, healthcare and training programmes continues today as this work has been passed over to the Chinese men and women whom we have trained to administer and lovingly operate these ventures. As long as we have continued faithful in prayer, trust and integrity with a willingness to stay open to the Holy Spirit and step forward in faith, we have proved that "Jesus Christ is the same yesterday and today and forever" (Hebrews 13:8).

In the development of any work of God it is imperative not to lose the emphasis on prayer and seeking direction by the Holy Spirit. Under the leadership of Moses, the children of Israel stayed close to the presence of God, symbolised by the cloud covering the Tent of Meeting. They only moved whenever it lifted and moved on (Exodus 40:36). We too need to have both a flexibility, a willingness to relinquish previous operations as the presence of God is lifted, as well as a determination to persevere in what God has initiated and called us to do, however hard the task is (Romans 4:20-21).

Over the years the centre of our operations in China moved from the south of the country northwards as doors were opened into state welfare centres. During the early stages of caring for abandoned children the emphasis was on caring for babies but as children grew older, those who were not adopted needed education, rehabilitation and medical care. We also discovered children with special needs who had not been abandoned, cared for by parents in desperate need of support and specialist help. To meet these needs and others in the community there had to be a growing emphasis on training local staff with input from qualified overseas volunteers.

The costs involved in these programmes involving hundreds of children and staff members were and continue to be enormous but God is faithful. At the same time we have continued until the devastating impact of the Covid pandemic to recruit men and women from around the world who are willing to teach English in academic institutions in various locations. With the growth of the work in China there has been a parallel growth of support organisations overseas with people committed to praying and supporting the work financially. Looking back to the initial vision which Gabrielle had received in Colchester in 1974 and our early steps of faith, walking the streets of China in the years that followed, trusting God for doors to open, we can only stand back in awe as we consider His faithfulness and creative power with the rapid growth, development and diversity of the work in the years that followed. As we shared earlier, flexibility in the work of God is vital as the apostle Paul and his co-workers realised on their second missionary journey (Acts 16:7).

In 2009 Gabrielle fell suddenly ill with a heart problem in a city in north China where we had made our home and was the centre of operations for all our programmes. With difficulty we succeeded in returning to England where it became obvious that she would not be able to travel to the Far East again. Cyril continued making regular visits to China to oversee the work but within three years the Lord had made it clear that we were to hand on our responsibilities to faithful men and women, both Western and Chinese who had joined us in the work. Although we would continue to support our brothers and sisters in the work in China which thrives today in spite of increasing government control, the door was closing for us there. God wanted us to be available to go through the next door that would be opened for us, a change of location from the Far East to the far west of Ireland.

We praise God that He continues to lead and speak prophetically, and that as we abandon ourselves to His sovereign plans for our lives, He will make provision for all our needs and renew us daily in the life of His Spirit. "Those who hope in the Lord will renew their strength. They will soar on wings like eagles; they will run and not be weary, they will walk and not be faint." (Isaiah 40:31)

Part Two

Prophecy and Application

"Do not merely listen to the word, and so deceive yourselves. Do what it says. Anyone who listens to the word but does not do what it says is like a man who looks at his face in a mirror and, after looking at himself, goes away and immediately forgets what he looks like." (James 1:22- 24)

"I have chosen you and equipped you that you should go and bring forth fruit. There will always be choices before you and paths that look appealing but my choice for you, my servants, is that you should travel along pathways that are fruitful. Do let a wrong sense of duty and conscientiousness delude you and cause you to remain trudging along wearily in courses of action that look highly commendable but do not bring forth fruit. As long as you remain in these courses of action, you will experience increasing frustration and tiredness because you have chosen your way instead of waiting for Me to direct your future. Get out of bondage to what seem to be good courses of action that are determined by a desire to please others and take only those courses of action that are chosen by Me for I have shaped your life and I know what will provide fulfilment for the gifting that I have placed within you. Choose My ways however unattractive or misunderstood they may seem to be for, in so doing, you will choose the way of fruitfulness and the way that will generate life within you."

After receiving our call to China some years earlier, we subsequently stepped out in faith to prepare for the fulfilment of that call; Cyril resigned from his salaried position and enrolled in a theological college in the south of England where he studied for ministry from 1979 to 1981. Different ways opened before us. We could have taken the role of ordination within the denomination to which the college belonged. This was an attractive proposition as we had four teenage children and had lost our salaried income; the denomination is large and ministry within it offered great security for one's working life and a pension to follow. Even more appealing was acceptance by its global mission society with a very sound administrative and financial base.

Appealing and reasonable as these courses of action appeared, the reality was that they did not necessarily open the way for us to go to China. Graduating from the college with all our finances exhausted and no clear plan for fulfilling our call to China was challenging, particularly as all of Cyril's fellow theological students were being ordained and moving on into ministerial positions in well-established churches. Prayerfully we waited on God, allowing His grace to propel us forward along the way of complete surrender to His will and call upon our lives. Selling all our limited possessions enabled us to buy one-way air tickets to Hong Kong for our family. We did not know where we would sleep, what we would eat and what we would do, but God is faithful. The pathway of surrender to God's will and call is the pathway of liberation and fruitfulness. We praise Him for all the abundance of fruit that followed as we continued along that pathway of obedience.

Preparing for Battle

"These are significant times. The battle lines are being drawn up and the sound of preparation for battle is being heard. The sound of the first cannons firing stirs the soldiers gathering their weapons as they hurry to join the ranks of those waiting to be summoned into the conflict. This is not a time to be going about one's own business indifferent to the spiritual challenges around. It is time to wake up to the call of the trumpet and prepare for the battle ahead. There is no place for civilians here; all are being summoned to join the lines for battle. Wake up. Wake up. How long will you avert your gaze from the what is happening around you? Every warrior will be needed and expected to commit himself to the battle that is to come."

When we were baptised in the Holy Spirit in 1973 we both experienced a deep sense of the Lord's presence within and a joy that strengthened us. At last Cyril felt the power of the Holy Spirit in his life, the power to maintain a consistent Christian testimony and to walk in holiness while working in a very secular environment. One of his thoughts, on arriving at this place, was that we should aim for a "balanced" life, avoiding going to extremes and giving offence to anyone. Gabrielle could see clearly that this was not to be the case: there needed to be absolute commitment to the Lord Jesus

Christ if we were to remain close to Him. Battles followed quickly with conflicts raging at times as Cyril took a strong stand for righteousness in the work place. It was imperative that we stood back to back protecting one another, praying for each other, as enemy forces often swept against us. There were attempts at times to undermine what we were doing in the Lord's name and to remove us from that location but God is our commander in chief. He will not allow the righteous to be moved. As long as we are fully committed to Him and standing in the place chosen for us in the battle, we shall be safe and under the protection of the rock of ages.

Letting go of the problems

"It can be very easy to hold onto difficulties and problems which in themselves provide a security and frame work to shape your days. They can be the focus for your thoughts and activities, often attracting sympathy from others while preventing you from stepping forward into uncharted territory where unknown challenges await you. Even your prayer life can be a predictable rehearsing of difficulties and passive acceptance; anything positive and victorious is seldom heard from your lips. Take hold of the victory that Christ has won for you on the cross and His splendid resurrection, and start believing and planning for answers. Many of your concerns and fears are in your mind and can be blown away as you start to pray positively, declaring that He will open a way for you. And be prepared to step forward along that way as it is revealed to you. You must be willing to let go of past patterns of self-pitying thoughts, and embrace the new challenges and responsibilities that will seem daunting at times as you leave the shadows where you have hidden for too long. You may feel very exposed in the bright sunlight but this is the place of freedom where you will be enabled to be released as you depend on the word of God and experience life in the Spirit."

In 1981 when we first arrived on Lamma, an outlying island in Hong Kong, to set up home for ourselves and three teenage children, we were the only westerners in a traditional fishing community. Our possessions were minimal and we had very limited resources so our life style was simpler than the local Chinese many of whom were prospering running popular seafood restaurants. Friends very kindly allowed us to camp out living on the ground floor of a three-storey house which they had started to rent. It felt very temporary as we and our children had to sleep on mattresses on the floor. We needed our own home.

One day arriving back at the island on the simple wooden ferry which linked us to the south of densely populated, fast-moving Hong Kong Island, Gabrielle's attention was drawn to one of the two-storey shabby buildings on the waterfront. She told Cyril that there were Chinese characters written on it which would confirm that this building was where God would have us live. It took the sceptical Cyril some time to concede eventually that there were indeed Chinese characters which could be barely discerned beneath the dirty white paint covering the building.

We were amazed to discover that the characters were the name of a gospel hall which had once occupied the premises many years previously. On viewing the upper floor of the building, Cyril became even more sceptical as it was in a very dilapidated condition having previously been a working men's dormitory. There was no bathroom apart from a filthy toilet;

nor was there any separate accommodation apart from two tiny rooms at the back.

The landlord was not keen to rent the upper floor to us because the local villagers were very superstitious, bound by fear of offending local spirits and not wanting to upset them by having a Christian family living there. The rent was excessive and really beyond our means, and negotiations with the landlord became more difficult. It would have been so easy to have held on to the difficulties we had of trying to make the best of camping out as a family on somebody else's ground floor.

Attempting to move to the dilapidated former men's dormitory would mean more confrontation with the Chinese landlord, finding more money to pay the rent each month, and having to renovate and adapt the premises to create a home for us and our teenage children. We praise God that the Lord challenged Cyril to trust Him and press forward to adopt a very positive attitude to the landlord, thereby securing a rental agreement. We were also given the faith to rely on God for the means and ability to convert the premises into what became an acceptable home for the next year and a half. We never lacked the dollars to pay each month's rent and the home became an effective place for ministry to both local Chinese villagers and international visitors.

Holy Ground

"As you open your heart and mouth in praise and worship, you will become increasingly aware of My presence and a growing realisation that you are coming onto ground that is holy. This is a sacred place reserved for those who are willing to walk in holiness and absolute obedience to My will. Only proceed if you are willing for My spirit to do a radical work in your life. To move in depths of praise and worship is not a casual experience to be entered into as an occasional pursuit to add some colour to one's spiritual life. These depths contain the essence of life itself where My power is active and where I desire to communicate with you at the deepest level of your being. You cannot afford to hold onto anything that is tainted and unworthy of a life lived in surrender to My will. You can only continue to stay on this holy ground if you know that your desire is to have hands that are clean and a heart that is pure."

Following our being baptised in the Holy Spirit in Hong Kong in 1973 we experienced initially great joy and also excitement as we were enabled with the releasing that the gift of tongues brings to enjoy times together worshipping and praising God. There quickly followed then a season of coming under the discipleship of the Holy Spirit. There needed to be a work of cleansing in both of our lives. We had followed our own ways, sometimes falling into sin and deceiving one another. Everything had to be brought to the light. Past failures had to be confessed to the other partner. We had to learn to forgive one another and trust the Lord for the healing of deep hurts. The holy place is a place of healing, cleansing and restoration. We vowed to live lives that were open and transparent, concealing nothing from each other. It was on this foundation of truth that the Lord was able to rebuild our marriage and call us to a life of service for Him.

"There is nothing to stop you moving forward except what is within you which prevents you from abandoning yourself to God and His purpose for your life. Go. You have hesitated too long and allowed yourself to sink deeper into confusion, doubt and despair. My way is always a way of fulfilment, and, as you take steps forward in obedience to Me in the direction which I show you, strength will rise within you. Moving forward in My direction for you is always a positive way. Negativity is not part of my plans which are always to bless and bring life. Do not hold back any longer but make the decision that you know you should make. You have allowed uncertainty and fear of the unknown to paralyse your will and determination to fulfil my purpose for you. Standing still will engulf you with weakness and frustration. Go forward and experience life, joy and fulfilment."

It would have been so easy to have justified waiting for years before stepping out in obedience to the vision which God had given to us for serving Him in China. If Cyril had stayed five more years in his job he would have been entitled to a pension. Our teenage children were all at school or college and, with Cyril's job, there came generous provision with educational allowances. Gabrielle's elderly mother was facing some health problems. We were already involved in ministry in our free time. The future in China could not be predicted as it had been closed to missionaries and most foreigners since the Communist revolution in 1949. However, the call of God was clear and the conviction that our response should not be delayed. We knew that we had to go even though it meant taking our three youngest teenage children out of all education, selling the last of our possessions and buying one-way air tickets to Hong Kong. We had virtually no money left, no promises of support and no idea where we would live or what we would do but God had spoken. That was sufficient. Jesus is the same, yesterday, today and forever. He was able to provide for all of our needs and He did even though we faced challenge after challenge.

Our children were wonderful: they were united with us in stepping out in faith to fulfil what God had called us to do; they actually eventually went on to experience academic achievements, successful marriages and fulfilling jobs. Gabrielle's mother, who was very supportive of our decision even though she was not a believer, continued to enjoy another ten years of good health. On arriving in the People's Republic of China, we realised why it had been so important not to delay. The new leadership was determined that the nation should embark on the road to modernisation and it was necessary to open the doors to foreign experts who could provide the English language skills to help Chinese professionals connect with the outside world. An effective door for service opened and there could be no delay in taking the opportunity to share the good news.

Come to the River

"The river is flowing,
The river of God is flowing deep and strong,
A river of love flowing from the throne of God;
O come to the river.
What is holding you back?
There's nothing to fear as you plunge on in,
A river of silver and the richness of gold,
A golden river, burning with the love of God.
O come to the river.
Let go of sin.
Feel the depth of His mercy
As you plunge within,
The mercy of God and the vastness of love,
The love of God's presence flowing from Him."

When the Lord opened the door for us to start work in the mainland of China in 1982, we were determined that whatever we did was in response to the direction of the Holy Spirit. We did not want the work of God to be encumbered with the burden and restrictions that seemed so often to be the case with being part of an organisation with structures and hierarchies. It seemed to us that all too often what had begun as an outpouring of the Holy Spirit, was subsequently lost as people established organisations to protect and develop the work that had been started

Within a year, we discovered that in order to be able to have any meaningful presence and credibility in a communist country, where thinking was dominated by collectivism rather than individualism, we needed to establish an organisation. This would be needed to make the arrangements to care for all our co-workers whom the Lord would send from around the world. The challenge was always to stay within the river of life, sensitive to the Holy Spirit, and not to allow the demands of maintaining an organisation, with its inevitable financial and personnel pressures, to undermine truth, integrity and faithfulness to the word of God and the direction of His Spirit.

Way of Escape

"You cannot see the way forward. You seem to be blocked in and there is no way of resolving all the difficulties and challenges facing you. Prayers seem to be unanswered. It is I who have brought you to this place where the problems seem insurmountable. As you bring everything to Me, handing over the entire situation and the trials which you are facing, I shall reveal the key to open the door which will provide the way of escape. It will not be the way which you would have chosen but it is my chosen pathway for you. It is because you are so desperate that you will be willing to take this opportunity. I have had to bring you to this place of trial with all its challenges to give you no other option than to take the way of escape. As you venture along this pathway, which is my plan for you, you will find fulfilment and freshness as you explore what I have prepared for you." (I Corinthians 10:13)

In 1985 Cyril and a colleague travelled to two cities in southern China visiting universities anxious to recruit overseas teachers of English to equip their students who needed to relate to the world outside of China which had been closed for many years. They carried with them a number of applications from well-qualified teachers, so they approached negotiations with the university authorities with a great sense of optimism that good placements could be found. To their dismay one by one the doors closed and by the time they returned to the office in Hong Kong not one teaching position had been found for the overseas volunteers who were already preparing to leave their home countries and travel to China. The doors had all closed.

Cyril and Gabrielle were forced to travel further afield to remote regions of China to look for new opportunities. As they met university authorities in these regions and were warmly welcomed, it was obvious that God wanted us to move our main focus away from the south of the country, where we had grown to be comfortable, to extend our work with universities and colleges across this vast nation. New doors opened and the number of teachers increased. What had seemed to be a closed door was, in fact, the Lord's "way of escape" to force us to move out of our comfort zone and into His much wider purposes.

The Danger of Drifting

"You must realise that it is imperative that you know My direction for your life, that you are aware of the danger of drifting when you are not clear about My purpose for you. It is only when you are fully yielded to Me, abandoned to My will, that direction will be clear. Without that clarity you are like a boat drifting on the ocean, blown here and there by winds and moved by random currents, with no destination to head for. I want you to move out of frustration and purposeless into My plan for your life. It is only as you grasp My plan and are determined to fulfil it that you shall know peace and the satisfaction that comes from being in My will and not drifting in vagueness and uncertainty."

After returning to Hong Kong in 1981 as missionaries living by faith, trusting in the faithfulness of God to provide for all the needs of our family, we were very quickly led to join a slightly older missionary couple who had considerable experience of ministry in several countries. Within a few weeks we moved to an outlying island to establish a base for mission across Asia as well as local ministry. The Holy Spirit moved swiftly and within the space of about six months, we established a local church, a training programme for ministry and outreach programmes. Sadly there were tensions in our relationship with the other couple which exploded after two years resulting in a devastating split in the work. We felt numb and confused not knowing the way forward. We stood aside and let the other couple take most of the work in the direction which they believed was right. This left us with responsibility for the work in mainland China which we had been pioneering, a growing work as more people from overseas responded to the opportunity to share the love of God while employed as teachers in China.

Cyril particularly felt a reluctance to give himself fully to this work as it meant dropping our missionary identity which was fine in Hong Kong but unacceptable in Communist mainland China. It was very important for us to be regarded by the Communist Chinese authorities as professional academics. Cyril had previously abandoned his professional career in the United Kingdom to serve the Lord as a faith missionary. Now it seemed that he must abandon this identity to move in academic circles in order to advance the work in China. We would still be trusting the Lord to provide for all our needs but to the outside world we would appear to be pursuing professional goals. As long as Cyril wrestled with the Lord over what He was clearly calling us to do, there was confusion and uncertainty. Peace and breakthrough came as he laid down all claims to fulfilling his own desires and missionary status, and instead put His trust in the Lord and obeyed His direction for opening academic and professional doors in China.

Move Forward in Victory

"I have called you to victory,

To know the trumpet call that will summon you to battle.

You are called to move in faith,

To know the triumph of the overcomer.

As you look not at the circumstances but to Me

And step boldly forward declaring the word of the Lord,

Believing in the promises of your God,

So you shall never be defeated but will sing the song of the victorious in battle.

Rise up, rise up, and believe My word.

Do not allow the enemy to paralyse you with doubt and fear.

Let my Holy Spirit fill you with hope and trust in your God.

Declare with your lips My promises to you,

Then step forward in confidence in My word to you

In victory, My beloved, knowing a life of triumph,

The joy of the overcomer, life to the full in Me."

In pioneering a work to proclaim the good news of God's redeeming love through professional work in China, we encountered many challenges and setbacks. In order to support the needs of a growing team of teachers from several overseas countries in different locations across the vast Chinese mainland, it was necessary to maintain an effective office in Hong Kong. Sound administration was vital, undertaken by a small team of dedicated colleagues to support the teachers and families out on the field.

We needed to work together in harmony, to enjoy fellowship and to grow in mutual trust and respect for one another. With all the difficulties of trying to work with Communist Party officials in China, we needed to experience a flow of prayer and the power of the Holy Spirit. One of the most discouraging experiences was to be told suddenly that a team member, who seemed to be committed to the work, had decided to leave and move on to do something else. Plans involving personnel across China and future development could be suddenly thrown in jeopardy. We discovered that it was vital on these occasions not to succumb to defeat and despair but to move in victory, praising God and declaring that His purposes would stand for us, China and the work. We praise God as we recall that we never lacked people to work with us; even though we faced disappointment with every departure yet the Lord always brought in others, usually more gifted and better able to do the work and flow in with the rest of the team.

The Army of God

"I am raising up an army. This is not a time for taking one's ease and relaxation. Increased vigilance is needed if the hostile forces rising up within the land are to be defeated. Gird up the loins of your mind and prepare for battle. The enemy is vicious, and subtle and deceptive. Grasp hold of the urgency of the hour. The battle is a spiritual one so spiritual weapons are needed. Wisdom and discernment are needed so that you are united with others who also have a passion for prayer, truth and righteousness."

In 1987 from our base in Hong Kong we were delighted to be able to send our first team to an ancient city in central China. The previous year God had opened a door in one of the universities in the city and we had been able to provide a young English woman to teach language students. She had made a favourable impression with the authorities who asked if we could provide more teachers. As we gathered to pray for the team before they embarked on the long overnight train journey from Guangzhou to the ancient city, we were given a remarkable prophetic word. The ancient city is one of the great walled cities of the world just like the ancient city of Jericho which was taken by the children of Israel under Joshua. We were told that this ancient Chinese city, like Jericho, would only be taken for the Lord through praise and unity. We were very encouraged by the word and settled the new team into their university with a great sense of expectation.

Sadly within months team unity was shattered and there was muted praise. Indeed it took new teams in the following years some time to establish and preserve unity, which was often under attack but the battle was won for the Lord. Continuing praise and openness to the gifts of the Holy Spirit were important keys to expanding and developing the work throughout the city and province. It was with great joy that we saw an abundance of fruit resulting from the foundation of unity and praise.

Do not fear to take My way

"Do not fear to take My way. You need to move ahead with trust and unquestioning obedience for I have chosen the way for you however unlikely it may seem or at times unreasonable. Don't question my direction and the way that I am laying out before you. All that I ask of you is that you step out on the way that I am showing you. Don't question. Simply trust your Father. As I have chosen the way before you so I shall bless you as you take steps of faith along that way. In that way alone you will find fulfilment, joy and peace for your soul."

It seemed very unreasonable when God made it very clear to us that we should give up our home in Hong Kong in 1994. Thirteen years earlier when we had stepped out in faith from England in obedience to His call to China, the Lord had led us to take up residence on Lamma, a small island south of the main Hong Kong Island. There we had faced many challenges as we established an office and base for the work across China. We had made friends too with the local Chinese community among whom we were able to share the love of God and the good news of Jesus Christ. We believed that we were there to stay indefinitely, experiencing great fulfilment as we lived and worked in a simple Chinese village.

As circumstances made it increasingly clear that to continue resisting the will of God was foolish and irresponsible, we realised that God was leading us back to England where he provided a home for us. God is faithful: in our journey of faith we had not been able to save any money but wonderfully we were enabled to put down a deposit and obtain a mortgage to buy a small apartment. From this location we were able to travel to other nations to share about the work in China which from 1994 expanded to include programmes involving childcare and healthcare. Volunteers, many of them professional specialists, were needed to facilitate this work as well as large funds to ensure the wellbeing of the children in our care. It was important that we handed over to others the day-to-day management of the office in Hong Kong and work in China so that we could be free to develop the work internationally as well spending more time in mainland China.

You are called to be a warrior for God

"I am calling you to be a warrior at this time for the battle is intense, and I need those whom I call to be prepared to follow My orders in the battle. Do not go your own way or listen to others for I alone know what must be done. Do not let yourself be intimidated but be the warrior that I have designed you to be and shout forth the praises of your God."

One of the greatest challenges facing us as we developed our work in China was our ongoing need for fellowship, accountability and support. The last thing that we wanted was to be independent mavericks following our own agenda. The need increased as the work grew and we carried responsibility for Christian volunteers from various nations who had been called to serve the Lord in China.

We needed to be accountable especially when differences of opinions arose between ourselves and those serving with us. As the work grew so did the enormous financial commitment to provide ongoing twenty-four-hour care for abandoned children in our homes in China. There were times when we felt very encouraged when organisations in English-speaking countries took an interest in our work, providing volunteers and financial support.

Sadly often pressure came too from such organisations to become part of their systems or face the prospect of losing their volunteers and financial support. We knew that God had raised up our work to be inter-denominational, to be a channel and resource available to the whole body of Christ. On these occasions as financial needs increased and support was withdrawn so did the realisation that we were to be warriors who had been called to battle to see God's purposes fulfilled in China. God is faithful and we are thankful that the growing work in China never lacked whatever finance was needed and dedicated staff to ensure that all responsibilities were fulfilled.

You have a choice

"Truly this is a season when I am pouring out My spirit again and there is a fresh move of your God taking place. I am giving you the opportunity to be a part of what I am doing in this new day. I shall not force you for I shall never compel anyone who is unwilling to respond to the work of My spirit. You have a choice. The decision is yours: to ask the Holy Spirit to fill you and take you forward in My purposes where you abandon yourself to My will for your life. Abandonment to My spirit is costly but only in this way will you experience the fullness of My blessing and the outworking of all that I have planned for you and destined you to be."

We came to realise in our work in Hong Kong and China that many if not most Christian missions were closed to the operation of gifts of the Holy Spirit. Prayer times with other missionaries could be very quiet meetings. It would have been very easy to water down what the Holy Spirit had done within us to make ourselves more acceptable to other Christians. Our organisation was unusual in having regular times of enthusiastic prayer, waiting on the Lord, expecting God to speak through tongues and interpretation as well as prophecy.

The tendency is always for the fire of revival to be allowed to burn itself out and for something safer, more comfortable and predictable to replace it. We were determined not to resist the work of the Holy Spirit but to abandon ourselves to however the Holy Spirit chose to operate and whatever He commissioned us to do.

Trust Me at all times

"It is my desire that you should know My peace, to be able to rest in that peace whatever the challenges and uncertainties that you are facing. It is not My desire that you should be burdened with trying to work out solutions and ways forward, anxiously anticipating what may or may not be the outcomes. Anxiety will only lead to doubt, fear and increasing confusion. You must learn to put your trust in Me, confident that I have already prepared the solution and the way forward. You must abandon your thoughts and your ways, and rest in Me so that you will see the outworking of My thoughts and My ways. As you trust Me so My peace will fill you and a joy will begin to rise within you. Your name is written on the palms of My hands and My intention at all times is that you will be in a place of rich fulfilment and blessing."

As the work which we had started in China grew and developed with increasing responsibilities for needy children and vulnerable young adults, it was important that we should consider how we could ensure that the work would be sustained in future years. We were growing older too and questions were raised by our international board members regarding the plan for succession. Who would be willing and equipped to take on our roles one day and oversee the various programmes as well as ensuring that our local Chinese staff members were cared for and practical necessities like salaries and pension plans were properly managed? As the years slipped by, various succession plans were considered, some of which looked very reasonable from a human perspective but none of which seemed to quite work out. As we learned to rest in God and trust Him for His plans to be outworked, it was amazing to see how He had prepared our local Chinese managers to take on the responsibilities and develop the work in ways that we had not considered. The old hymn, "Trust and obey," is as relevant in today's technological world as ever.

Part Three

Radical Living

"My lover spoke and said to me, 'Arise, my darling, my beautiful one, and come away with me. See! The winter is past: the rains are over and gone. Flowers appear on the earth; the season of singing has come.'" (Song of Songs 2:10-12)

"I want you to come close to My heart. Draw near, My beloved, for it is as you come closer to Me that you will feel the heartbeat of My love. This is a journey of the heart, of your heart becoming one with My heart. A decision of will is needed: to move from where you are to come alongside the heart of Jesus. This is truly the place of rest that you long to know. Move now, come closer to My heart and experience My peace.

"For I am indeed calling out a people who shall not only know the high praises of their God, but a people who will move in absolute obedience to My will. For I am looking for those whose hearts are perfect towards Me, perfect in the sense that their hearts are wholly given to Me; and if you will truly give yourself wholly to Me then you shall know My perfect will for your life. For I am in these days indeed doing a radical work and I'm looking for those who are willing to be a radical people, a people transformed by My Spirit and My love, and willing to walk in that pathway, that narrow pathway, of absolute obedience to My will. So, search your heart this day and ask yourself, 'Am I willing to give myself wholly and surrender my will and every part of my being to the Lord my God that I might know the fullness of His will in my life?'

"God has been with you throughout your entire life. During the times of darkness and despair He has been there. He knows all about the difficult times and there is nothing hidden from Him. He knows you when you are at your weakest and He loves you with an intensity that you will never be able to fathom. He has brought you to this moment of time which can be a time of breakthrough now. As you set your will to praise Him and speak aloud your love for Jesus, your life can be transformed. It's time to take off the heavy cloak of mourning and put on the garment of praise. Praise needs to be vocal: as you lift your voice so you will break free and the chains will fall off.

"There is an opening now into the courts of praise, a place of entry into a depth of encounter with the Holy Spirit. It is available now if you are willing to abandon yourself to worship and praise directed and sustained by the Spirit of God. Deep calls to deep. You have spent too much time in the spiritual shallows where the sense of frustration is stifling the life that you still have. Simply come as you are and give yourself to the praise of your God, not trying to work out what is happening but come deeper into the heart of your God who will take you beyond the mental plane into a rich place of fulfilment. The courts of praise are where the journey begins into the progressive unfolding of what God has destined for your life.

"Deep still calls to deep in the roar of the waterfalls (Psalm 42:7). It is in the deep place of your being that you will begin to respond to the call of the Holy Spirit and start to move into the depths of God. God is wanting to open up depths within you. The difficulties and challenges that you face have been the tools that God is using to carve out a deeper place within you. Do not resist the work that He is doing so that your spirit can call out to His Spirit, where there can be a flow of spirit to spirit. There are depths within you still waiting to be plumbed and opened up to the Spirit of God which will reveal more of Him and more of you.

"There have been times when you have resisted the work of God in your life as He has sought to shape your life like a potter working with clay. His hand has seemed hard upon you because you have resisted what He has wanted to do. His desire is to shape you so that that you become a vessel that He can use. And when He has shaped you into the vessel that He has created you to be, do not be disappointed that there is a season when you are left on the shelf until the master potter knows when you are ready to be taken up again and put into the furnace. In that fiery place you will be made strong enough for all that will face you when His work of preparation is complete. Only then will you have the stamina and resources within you for the work that He has destined for you.

"You have started on a journey, an exciting journey, and it is important that you keep moving forward. This is not a time for hesitation but a time for stepping forward, trusting in My love for you, that my plans are to bless you and to bring you into a place of fulfilment, joy and abundance. Do not allow what is behind you, the dark times and troubled seasons, to occupy your attention but turn around and look ahead, not allowing doubt and fear to hold you back, a prisoner to what you have been in the past. Each step you take will increase your confidence in the direction in which I am taking you. Your steps of faith will be contested but every challenge overcome will bring strength to your soul and firmness to your character.

"The Holy Spirit is hovering over your life, searching the depths of your being to bring forth hidden treasures. There are depths within you which are waiting to be explored and brought into the light. Only the Holy Spirit can unlock that which is hidden within you. As you allow your spirit to be set free by the Spirit of God there shall come about a freedom and a willingness to let go of insecurities that have bound you and caused you to retreat beneath a protective layer. As long as you stay cocooned under this protective layer, your true self, your real self, is bound by inhibition and a fear of revealing who you really are. Surrender to the Holy Spirit who intends no harm but only wants to unwrap the outer layers and bring you into the light. The darkness is no place to hide and will harm your spirit. As you surrender and allow My Spirit to fill you with light so the treasure within you can be seen and can bless those who know you but have never had the opportunity to encounter the real you.

"Are you willing to let go of all those plans and projections and aspirations that you have, and abandon them and submit them to Me, and let me form My plans and My thoughts and My ways within you? I would have you come, as it were, with a clean slate, with an open heart, with an open book, an open page, that I may write upon your heart what is on My heart, that you might walk in My ways and know My thoughts and know My plans. I desire for you to move into a much higher orbit, onto a much higher plane, where you are living out My thoughts, My ways, My plans. For as you live in that dimension so you shall know the fulfilment that you desire. You shall know that sense of wellbeing, you shall know My joy, My peace, so that as you let go and surrender your thoughts, your plans, your ways, and allow Me to reveal My thoughts and plans to you and cause them to be birthed within you, then you shall know My life flowing through every part of you.

"You will be given such a sense of peace, and more than that, you will be given a sense of authority for the life is My life. For I am the light of the world, and as you obey My voice and, as you walk in that light, you will find so many things that have never changed before will change. It will not be because of what you are doing but it will be because of Me, because of My word that they will change. I say unto you, follow My word, listen to Me, walk in light and be that light yourself.

"For these indeed are days of great significance. I would have you know that decisions you make and how you spend your time and where you go and when you go, these are decisions that are very important during this time of significance. Do not miss out on what I want to do in your life. Do not miss out on what I want to do deep within you and through you. It is as you grasp the importance of how you must stay close to me, how you must listen to My voice, and only move and do those things that I show you to do, that you shall move in the centre of the significance of these days. I want to make your days significant. I want to make your thoughts significant. I want you to know My thoughts, My ways, to feel Me breathing the breath of God through you. Don't fail in these days to grasp the significance of what I am doing. Be in that place where I can take you deeper into Me and cause you to be a channel of My love in this place.

"I am the everlasting light. You will know that you are walking in My way as long as you stay in the light. Outside of that light is darkness and confusion. Remember that I am the creator of light and order. When you sense confusion and turmoil rising within then recognise that you are in danger and you must take active steps to move out of the place of confusion and return to the place of light. You will know that you are walking in the light again by the peace that fills your being even in times of stress, challenge and concern. Others around you may fail and fall but you will be protected by the light within, that light that floods the depths of your being. I am the light and in Me is no darkness at all. Do not let anyone or anything deceive you and beguile you into taking courses of action that look attractive and reasonable but cause darkness and confusion to rob you of your peace.

"It is only as you praise My name that you will be set free. I have ordained praise as a gift for you. It is My gift for you because, if you open your lips and open your heart to praise Me, you will find release, you will find freedom, you will find joy, you will find peace. So, set your heart, set your will to praise Me because in praising Me you will set yourself free.

"You are my precious jewel. You must not disparage yourself for in My sight you are of immense worth. Never doubt the intensity of My love for you. There are times when your life will seem to be a complex kaleidoscope of many disparate elements, so complex and unrelated that you will find it impossible to hold them all together. Stop trying. I am like a master technician who knows where all the parts and pieces fit together even though it all seems impossible to unravel. Rest in Me. Don't attempt to work everything out and bring together all the seemingly unrelated elements. Rest in Me, in My master plan, in My ability to coordinate everything and bring all the parts together at the right time to a fulfilment that only I could arrange. In the midst of all the busyness and all that crowds in upon you as events, people and circumstances make their demands, remember to rest in Me. Look to Me. Feel My presence. Absorb My peace. It will be like a gentle flowing waterfall constantly filling your hours and days with a deep awareness that I am with you. As the waterfall flows downwards into the depth below so the pool deepens. In the same way I am doing an ever-deeper work within you in all the rush and pressure of circumstances that demand your attention as you stay open to Me, receiving My peace and stillness for your spirit.

"Live in victory. Living in victory means a life of developing positive attitudes, responding in faith to all the challenges and vicissitudes that confront you and cause you to respond naturally with despair and a sense of being overwhelmed. But you are called to respond supernaturally as an overcomer, not with a sense of defeat but in victory. And this is the victory that has overcome the world – your faith. (1 John 5:4)

"Put the trumpet to your lips and declare the word of the Lord. As you proclaim the word that I have given you, the promises that I have made to you, the assurances that I have entrusted you with, so you shall see the fulfilment of what has been shown you. As long as you withhold from declaring My word there will be a withholding from the manifestation of it. Speak it out. Declare it in Zion. As you proclaim the word of your God so you shall know wholeness and a sense of wellbeing, for you will be faithful in declaring what you know to be true and what has been revealed to you.

"Open yourself to My love and life. I want you to open the whole of yourself not just a part. Do not hold back. As you give yourself to Me so you shall feel My life and My love flooding your being. You have nothing to fear as you give yourself to Me. My love will bring healing and wholeness to all the wounded and damaged parts of yourself, even the hidden parts. Remember at all times that I love you, I have created you and I have redeemed you. As My love fills you, bringing you along the pathway to wholeness so you shall experience life, My life, life in ever increasing fullness and richness. You will be aware of expansion where there has been constriction, colour instead of drabness and victorious living replacing a constant feeling of failure. Open up. Open up completely to My love and life.

"During the times of stress and strain when you feel buffeted by storms without and uncertainties within, it is of paramount importance that your is soul is firmly anchored in Me. You need an anchor that will hold you steady when emotions fly upward in anxiety and sink downwards in despair. As you hold fast to Me and all that I have promised you so you shall not fall apart and drift away from Me. You will recognise instead that the storms of stress and strain will ultimately serve to strengthen your faith and trust in Me because your anchor has held you safe. Without an anchor for your feelings, thoughts and emotions, you will always be vulnerable when challenges confront you. Set your mind now to anchor your whole self in Me.

"Cast not away your confidence that you do not lose that great reward that I have prepared for you, My beloved. Keep on running the race. You have need of endurance. As you wait on Me, I will cause you to rise up, to rise up on wings of eagles. As you wait on Me you will be lifted up in the spirit, the sense of weariness will go. I want to strengthen you. I want to endue you with My power from on high. You have been born again to an eternal destiny. At times the sense of drabness, the sense of weariness, the sense of tiredness are the result of your longings to be moving in a different sphere, in the sphere of eternity. Hold onto that which I have given you. As you rise up on wings of eagles so you shall know a breakthrough in the spirit. You shall know an outpouring of My love. You shall see a new dimension of power. So wait on Me. Let My endurance fill you with new strength. I shall equip you for that which lies ahead. It shall be greater than what you have experienced hitherto.

"The Lord has lit a fire, an intense fire, a fire that is growing in intensity and heat. He is placing you in the fire. Do not seek to come out of the fire for within the fire the Lord is forging weapons, weapons that He shall wield to bring down enemy strongholds. Do not seek to come out of the fire, the fire that the Lord has made, the fire that the Lord has created in order to prepare you My servants for all that lies ahead, for the battles. He is forging His weapons, weapons of immense strength, for they need to pass through the fire to be made strong so that He can wield them with power and authority, knowing that they will not fail in the hour of battle. So, do not seek to leave the fire, do not seek to come out of the fire. Let the Lord do that work of forging, refining, purifying and strengthening that you might be a weapon in the hands of the Lord, a weapon in His hands of love, in His hands of authority, in His hands of power to bring down enemy strongholds.

"For the Lord would have you to search your heart, to consider those things and activities that take up your time and energy, and review them and bring them before Me, to consider those activities which have truly been born of the Spirit and are for My glory, and to consider those activities which are a drain upon your energy and time and are truly not of Me. I want you to live and move in life, and as you give yourself to those activities and pursuits within the boundaries that I have given you, you will know life, you will know energy, you will know freedom, you will know release and joy. So, consider those things and those activities in which you are involved, and give yourself to those that are truly born of My Spirit and have My hand of blessing upon them.

"Look! I am opening new pathways before you. As you see and consider the new openings and opportunities being placed before you, you need to recognise that it is I the Lord who am creating this new season. Actually, they are not really new pathways for they are the outworking and development of all that I have taken you through previously. Do not hesitate to move forward in that which you know in your spirit is My direction for you and do not question this direction because it is unexpected and seems to be something for which you were not prepared. In your spirit you know that it is from Me and I have prepared this next step for you to take. Do not look at the circumstances and try to calculate the outworking of what is involved because you are required to walk by faith not according to your own earthly wisdom. Do not question what I am doing and the direction in which I am propelling you. It will be a pathway of great blessing, and provision has been made for every step of the way.

"I am doing a new work in your midst. It is the work of My Holy Spirit. Do not seek to contain the work that I am doing. The new wine of the Spirit shall flow. Do not try to contain it or limit it. It is the fresh, new wine of My Holy Spirit. It shall come forth in abundance. I ask for obedience. I ask for trust, I ask for simple faith that you might receive that blessing that I am pouring into your lap. I am pouring out of the abundance of My Holy Spirit. Let My Holy Spirit flow forth, gush forth. Seek not to limit or contain or question but let the fresh wine of My Holy Spirit flow through you and out through you bringing life to the helpless, life to the hopeless, life to those who are in despair. You shall see miracles. You shall see transformations as My Holy Spirit flows with abundance through you and out through you.

"The trumpet is sounding. The trumpet is sounding. The trumpet is sounding for battle. Be prepared, my people. Be prepared, my people. There are forces of darkness gathering and I want my people to be ready for battle, for my people to be ready to move as a disciplined army, as a force mighty, strong with banners, holding onto the word of the Lord, going forth in perfect unity. Oh, my people you will need to know as you have never known before the voice, the direction of my Holy Spirit. You have often asked to be led by my Holy Spirit, and truly I shall lead you by my Spirit as you listen to me. As you wait on me so I shall lead you, so I shall direct you. You will need to let go of so much, of so many of your plans, your preferences, your priorities. They will have to go and you will have to surrender to my will, to know what my orders are, to know what my commands are, so that you are in the right place on the day of battle. So, take heed to the voice of my Spirit. Give time to listen to my voice. Do not allow yourself to be swayed by the opinions of others. Do not allow yourself to be drawn this way and that way but hold fast to that which I give you. Be not double minded but hold fast to the word that I give you and let go of every distraction however good the distraction may be that will prevent you from wholly and completely and unconditionally following the direction that I shall give you."

Part Four

Releasing the treasure within

"But we have this treasure in jars of clay to show that this all-surpassing power is from God and not from us" (2 Corinthians 4:7).

In the parable of hidden treasure Jesus told the story of a man who, on finding treasure hidden in a field, hides it again and then in his joy goes and sells everything that he has to buy the field to possess the treasure (Matthew 13:44). Centuries earlier the prophet Malachi spoke of the day when the Lord Almighty would make up His treasured possession from those who feared the Lord and honoured His name (Malachi 3:16-17). When God created Adam from the dust of the earth, He poured into Him the breath of His life, something to be treasured. It lay there hidden, concealed in man's earthiness, his sin-filled, fallen nature until Jesus came and gave everything He had, His life, to redeem men and women from all wickedness and purify for Himself a people that are His very own. We have been loved with an everlasting love (Jeremiah 31:3) and our Lord takes great delight in His treasured bride, rejoicing over us with singing (Zephaniah 3:17).

As transformed men and women, citizens of an eternal kingdom, God's new creation, we have within ourselves the Holy Spirit, the deposit from above guaranteeing what is to come (2 Corinthians 1:22). We are not to lose heart by dwelling on our weaknesses, fragility, disappointments, setbacks and struggles, all too aware that we carry this heavenly treasure within our very earthy natures. Often we may feel that our "jars of clay" are unworthy containers for the life of God, the treasure with which we have been entrusted (2 Corinthians 4:7). The apostle Paul encourages us by recalling the revelation that the grace of God is sufficient for us, that His power is made perfect in our weakness (2 Corinthians 12:9).

It is important that the treasure that we have received is not hidden away, something so precious that we conceal for fear of losing it. We have been given a spirit of boldness, not timidity, encouraged by the assurance that "the righteous are as bold as a lion" (Proverbs 28:1).

Each one of us has a unique testimony and calling in God who has put within us whatever gifts He has determined are most appropriate (1 Corinthians 12:11). Sadly, many Christians are restricted by an unhealthy self-consciousness, with a hyperawareness of their own weakness and seeming lack of ability. As a result gifts are locked within instead of being freely shared. We are meant to develop a generosity of spirit, a freedom in God, a big-heartedness that pervades the whole of our beings and enables us to be released as channels for the word of God in creative expressions of love that will bring blessing and encouragement to others (2 Corinthians 9:6).

In the wonderful account of the coming of the magi, the wise men from the east, to worship the one "who has been born king of the Jews" we are told that they brought treasures as an expression of their worship. On entering the house, their immediate response on seeing the infant Jesus with his mother, Mary, was to bow down and worship him. It is so important that we never lose a sense of awe and reverence in our worship. Significantly they then opened their treasures and presented their gifts (Matthew 2:11). The gifts, the treasure deposited within us, have to be opened and presented as an act of worship to our heavenly king. Some of us have stayed silent too long; the words of the lover in the Song of Songs are so descriptive of our bound, repressed condition:

"You are a garden locked up, my sister, my bride; you are a sealed fountain."

For us to become "a garden fountain, a well of flowing water streaming down from Lebanon", we need to cry out:

"Awake, north wind, and come, south wind. Blow upon my garden, that its fragrance may spread abroad" (Song of Songs 4:12,15-16).

When we are willing to cry out to the Holy Spirit to come and blow His life into us, our inhibitions can be released and the fragrance of the life of Jesus can be spread abroad through the gifts and fruit of the Holy Spirit.

The gifts that the wise men brought are powerful symbols of the life that flows within those who have been transformed by the new covenant that Jesus mediated (Hebrews 9:14-15). Gold speaks of obedience, the desire of the believer to submit everything to our Master, to continue moving forward in the life of faith – "of greater worth than gold, which perishes even though refined by fire" (1 Peter 1:7).

Myrrh, the precious spice used for embalming the body of Jesus after the crucifixion (John 19:39-40), speaks of the death of our old life of sin and our new freedom in Christ (Romans 6:4-7). Incense speaks of worship, prayer and intercession and it is in this area of Christian life and experience that we need to grow in order to experience greater intimacy with God and the life of the Spirit.

One outstanding feature over recent years in Limerick city in Ireland has been the concern demonstrated by Christians from a wide spectrum of backgrounds for a challenging housing estate. Every week, prior to the lockdown caused by the pandemic, a powerful evening of prayer, worship and proclamation took place on the estate with significant results. As the incense offering of prayer ascended from the heart of the estate so levels of violent crime descended. There is a spiritual battle being fought for the soul of Ireland and victory over the dark forces that blight so many lives can only be won as the lamps are lit and there is an offering to the Lord of "a perpetual incense" of prevailing prayer (Exodus 30:8).

The cry of the psalmist was: "Let my prayer be set before You as incense, the lifting up of my hands as the evening sacrifice" (Psalm 141:2). The incense offered up in the temple was prepared in obedience to the instructions given by God to Moses (Exodus 30:34-38). Our prayers are offered up to God as we pour out our hearts to Him but we need the divine, heaven-prepared anointing to take the cries pouring from our inmost being into the supernatural realm of God's awesome holiness. The lifting up of our hands will often be a sacrificial action, an act of obedience when emotionally we are feeling jagged and raw, but God will cause the sweet aroma of His presence to transform us and the situations that have distressed us.

The offering of incense in a twice-daily ritual was restricted under the old covenant to one place, the tabernacle or temple, by one person who had to be an anointed priest according to the order of Aaron. The prophet Malachi foresaw the time when the privilege of making an incense offering of prayer would be extended to any anointed member of the new covenant priesthood "according to the order of Melchizedek". There would be no restrictions of time or place to the spiritual sons of Levi who have been purified and purged as gold and silver "that they may offer to the Lord an offering in righteousness" (Malachi 3:3):

"'For from the rising of the sun even to its going down, My name shall be great among the Gentiles; in every place incense shall be offered in My name, and a pure offering; for

My name shall be great among the nations,' says the Lord of hosts." (Malachi 1:11).

It is imperative that we lay hold of the truth that we "are a chosen generation, a royal priesthood, a holy nation, His own special people" with splendid privileges and solemn responsibilities.

The glorious nature of the privileges entrusted to us is captured in the book of Revelation when the prophet is taken upward through the heavenly door and in the Spirit comes before the throne of God. Around the dazzling colours of the enthroned celestial being, surrounded by the emerald-like rainbow, are the four living celestial creatures and twenty-four elders with golden crowns, clothed in white robes, and sitting on thrones. When Jesus, the Lamb and the Lion of the tribe of Judah, takes the sealed scroll from the right hand of the Almighty, there is a dramatic response from both the four living creatures and the twenty-four elders which vividly portrays the power of the incense offering which combines worship and prayer:

"Now when He had taken the scroll, the four living creatures and the twenty-four elders fell before the Lamb, each having a harp, and golden bowls full of incense, which are the prayers of the saints." (Revelation 5:8)

The ministry of worship, praise and prayer, the offering of incense in purity, opens a door into the heavenly realm and releases powerful forces that will accomplish the will of God on earth:

"Then another angel, having a golden censer, came and stood at the altar. He was given much incense, that he should offer it with the prayers of all the saints upon the golden altar which was before the throne. And the smoke of the incense, with the prayers of the saints, ascended before God from the angel's hand. Then the angel took the incense, filled it with fire from the altar, and threw it to the earth. And there were noises, thunderings, lightnings and an earthquake." (Revelation 8:3-5)

The powerful symbolism of incense, with its pleasing aroma and smoke billowing upwards to heaven, is a graphic picture of prayer being made to God in an attitude of worship and awe from Spirit-filled, cleansed believers.

The incense used in the tabernacle was prepared according to divinely given instructions. This was a holy offering and the formula used in its preparation could not be used for any other purpose. The solemnity of these instructions reminds us that, in coming into the presence of God or exercising any of the gifts of the Holy Spirit, we are not to bring a mixture of self-promoting elements into our service to the Lord. Nor are we to take aspects of our ministry to the Lord and use them in other dimensions of daily life to influence or impress others. The word of God is very specific in its warning:

"But as for the incense which you shall make, you shall not make any for yourselves, according to its composition. It shall be holy for the Lord. Whoever makes any like it, to smell it, he shall be cut off from his people." (Exodus 30:37-38)

The ingredients used in the preparation of the special incense were to be found and gathered from the plants that grew in the wilderness through which the nation of Israel travelled in their long journey from Egypt to the promised land together with items purchased from traders. There was therefore a mixture of spices that were taken from ordinary herbs and costly materials that were much prized:

"And the Lord said to Moses: 'Take sweet spices, stacte and onycha and galbanum, and pure frankincense with these sweet spices; there shall be equal amounts of each.'" (Exodus 30:34)

The processes involved in obtaining the ingredients would have been varied and necessitated such methods as removing plants from their natural surroundings as well as burning, cutting or making incisions into the bark of trees. The wide range of ingredients is a wonderful picture of diversity within the body of Christ. God has called us from a vast spectrum of different backgrounds ranging from the poorest and dysfunctional to the highest echelons of society and privileged families to blend us together. There is a need for each ingredient, however seemingly insignificant, if the final product is to be perfectly formed. Aaron was commanded to burn "sweet incense" (Exodus 30:7) and the sweetness would not be the same without the presence of every spice.

The processes that the Lord uses before we can be fit for His use may be painful as activities, routines, relationships and pursuits which seemed an essential part of our lives previously will often have to be removed from us. What follows then can be yet more painful as we willingly submit to His dealings and processes which come from His Father's heart of love that desires to bring us to perfection and fulfilment:

"Now no chastening seems to be joyful for the present, but painful; nevertheless, afterward it yields the peaceable fruit of righteousness to those who have been trained by it" (Hebrews 12: 11).

Blending together so many diverse ingredients required tremendous skill in the same way that God brings together very different types of personality to form the body of Christ on earth. Dynamic life within the church becomes the norm when the people with different backgrounds, dispositions and strengths work together in unity:

"For as the body is one and has many members, but all the members of that body, being many, are one body, so also is Christ." (1 Corinthians 12:12)

Tension and disagreement in fellowships have been realties in church life from New Testament times but we need to recognise that God's purposes for His church, "which is His body, the fullness of Him who fills all in all" (Ephesians 1:23), will only be realised as we work through the challenges:

"Now I plead with you, brethren, by the name of our Lord Jesus Christ, that you all speak the same thing, and that there be no more divisions among you, but that you be perfectly joined together in the same mind and in the same judgment." (1 Corinthians 1:10)

As we set our minds to stay together in unity, to work through tensions and disagreements in love, honesty and transparency, so we shall encounter further processes in the hands of our divine Master to create the incense to be offered up to Him:

"And you shall make of these an incense, a compound according to the art of the perfumer, salted, pure, and holy. And you shall beat some of it very fine, and put some of it before the Testimony in the tabernacle of meeting where I will meet with you. It shall be most holy to you." (Exodus 30:35-36)

Salt is a symbol in scripture representing purity and the preserving power of holiness in daily life. In Old Testament times salt was associated with agreements so we find reference to "a covenant of salt forever before the Lord with you and your descendants with you" (Numbers 18:19).

It speaks of fidelity, perseverance in relationship and commitment, qualities that are sadly lacking in today's world. If we are to press on in discipleship to the Lord and fellowship with other believers, we shall need to persevere in honesty, humility and integrity in handling all that we are entrusted with, not wavering in our commitment to the Lord and His body. Jesus gave very specific warning about the danger of compromise and lowering standards in our Christian walk:

"You are the salt of the earth; but if the salt loses its flavour, how shall it be seasoned? It is then good for nothing but to be thrown out and trampled underfoot by men" (Matthew 5:13).

Likewise the emphasis on purity and holiness are essential if we are to experience intimacy in our relationship with the Lord and meaningful fellowship as well as deep, heartfelt friendship with other members of the body of Christ.

The command to "beat some of it very fine" is indicative of the fact that God is not concerned with something superficial that may have the appearance of being very religious but does not get down to the fine print of daily behaviour and attitudes. As the apostle Paul reminds us it is possible to be preoccupied with religious exercises which are completely ineffective in bringing us closer to God and enjoying freedom in Christ:

"These things indeed have an appearance of wisdom in self-imposed religion, false humility and neglect of the body, but are no value against the indulgence of the flesh" (Colossians 2:23).

To submit willingly to being disciplined by the Holy Spirit is to surrender one's own will, pride and prejudices and commit oneself to being real with God and those closest to us, to walking in the light, to letting go of self-promotion, to stop taking offence at perceived slights and to accepting criticism with a gracious spirit. Too often moves of the Holy Spirit in churches and fellowships have been brought to a standstill, not usually by doctrinal differences, but by personality clashes and competing egos. The first casualty when love, humility, purity, transparency, integrity and holiness are challenged is usually the prayer life of a church. There is a world of difference between perfunctory prayer and prayer powered by the Holy Spirit arising from lives of saints who are moving in holiness, obedience, compassion and integrity, offering upward a pleasing incense offering to God.

The incense which Aaron burnt before the Lord in the morning and evening was a "sweet incense". The fire was to be that which was authorised by God; to use "profane fire" (Leviticus 10: 1-3) was to bring destruction. When we come before the Lord our God in worship and prayer we must never forget that we are to "serve God acceptably with reverence and fear for our God is a consuming fire" (Hebrews 12:28-29). We cannot trivialise the sacred things of our Almighty God. He is, of course, always merciful, loving and ready to forgive as long as we are transparent, honest, truly repentant and trusting in His righteousness. The incense offering of prayer must ascend from pure hearts and clean hands (Psalm 24:3-4).

The truly outstanding feature of the life of a Spirit-filled believer is humility and servanthood. This was emphasised so often in the teaching of Jesus and the apostles:

"Your attitude should be the same as that of Christ Jesus, who, being in very nature God, did not consider equality with God something to be grasped, but made himself nothing, taking the very nature of a servant, being made in human likeness" (Philippians 2:5-7).

After the magi, the wise men, opened their treasure and presented the infant Jesus with their gifts, they quietly left Bethlehem and "returned to their country by another route" (Matthew 2:12). They heeded the warning given in a dream and avoided going to Jerusalem where Herod was waiting for news and where they had been the centre of attention previously. There is a warning there for us too. However much we may have been a blessing to others in exercising the gifts which God has given to us, it is imperative that we hear His "gentle whisper" (1 Kings 19:12) and not be caught up with the earthquake, wind and fire, the urge for something dramatic. We must be willing to move from being centre stage and quietly allow God to move us on to the place of His choosing.

Popularity, success and a desire to please others are very dangerous. God will allow our motivation to be tested so that it will become clear whether we are seeking to glorify Him or glorify ourselves. Our heart attitude and primary motivation must always be to stay close to our divine Master, to enjoy His presence and grow in relationship with Him. We have to be willing to acknowledge our limitations and to relinquish anything that will prevent us from growing in Him. Our calling is a heavenly one and our destiny is far beyond the confines of this earthly existence as Paul wrote in his letter to the church at Philippi:

"But one thing I do: forgetting what is behind and straining towards what is ahead, I press on towards the goal to win the prize for which God has called me heavenwards in Christ Jesus" (Philippians 3:13-14).

ABOUT THE AUTHORS

Cyril and Gabrielle Thomas met when they were studying at Nottingham University over sixty years ago. They married young and moved every few years with their growing family as Cyril pursued a career in education and training. A move to Hong Kong brought challenges which resulted in a lifetime of commitment to Christian discipleship and a journey of faith. The call of God which came in a vision took them to service in Communist China and outreach to students and abandoned children. They are living now in Ireland still seeking to be faithful to the word of God and direction by the Holy Spirit.

Printed in Great Britain
by Amazon

23569486R00066